RAIN SONGS

CRAIG RANDALL

Copyright © 2023 by Craig Randall
All rights reserved.
ISBN Ebook: 978-1-959510-88-8
ISBN Paperback: 978-1-959510-89-5
ISBN Hardcover: 978-1-959510-88-8
Cover Art by: @coverdungeondragon
Distributed by: Amazon KDP and Ingram Spark
Published by: Switchboard Publishing LLC
No part of this book may be reproduced in any form or by any electronic or mechanical means, including information storage and retrieval systems, without written permission from the author, except for the use of brief quotations in a book review.

ALSO BY CRAIG RANDALL

Fiction

The Doom that Came to Astoria: The Northwest Trilogy Part 1

The Dreams in the Pearl house: The Northwest Trilogy Part 2

Poetry

To Chase the Sun

Among the Wildflowers

DEDICATIONS

For Mary, Robert, Dylan, and D.H..

For my wife and children, who live this journey with me every day. I love you.

And for all who struggle and suffer (or ever have) with mental ailment(s). May we grow deeper in the undying strength within, and overcome.

"Be not afeared, the isle is full of noises, sounds and sweet airs, that give delight and hurt not."

William Shakespeare, *The Tempest*

INTRODUCTION

This collection is about disruption.

Disruption is uncomfortable. We don't like it. We like it when we make plans and our expectations play out and things flow. You know what I mean? Those *good days*?

I should note I was not expecting to write *this* collection of poems.

In 2018, I tried tapering off anxiety medication, and it went south. My mind cracked in half, and I entered one of the darkest periods of my life. Writing was an integral part of my recovery. Not merely the act of writing, though; writing intent on changing my thinking patterns. Writing with intention, to influence my thoughts and feelings.

It worked!

I was growing, learning, writing, *living*, really. Catapulting into a thought-life I never dreamed possible.

With *To Chase the Sun* I found hope again, and with *Among the Wildflowers* I learned how to cultivate and keep it. Or started to. So, as I wrote on, I expected it to land on some grand opus of a revelation about healing. Reaching the crescendo or high-point of peace and healing before gravity took its course and brought my feet back to the ground (in the positive, grounded sense of the word). I saw this peace with a longevity. Sustained.

Looking back, my assumptions seem foolish. Hindsight's such a blessing and a curse.

Looking back, I made *a plan*. In doing so, I created an expectation, and *when life happened*, it was obliterated.

Disruption.

All of this happened around 2019-2020.

Amidst bubbling global unrest, Covid struck.

So strange, as my world was coming together, the outside world crumbled. I used to joke that I was ahead of the curve. I'd spent the last year learning skills to cope with anxiety and depression, so I was ready.

Not for the fallout, though. Not for how long it lasted.

The weirdest thing about Covid, though, is how it affected us ALL. We each have a story, don't we? Experiences we think back on. Each of our different lives upended by our own versions of struggle.

I hoped that a common struggle would unite people more. Or blast open the doors for mental health, at least in America. It still may.

Either way, it laid waste to *our plans*. Didn't it? And we all lived in that strange *in-between*. For months-on-years. That ambiguous, unknown space. Discomforting and disorienting. Something most of us dislike. And now we're trying to rebuild those of us who can at least.

This period of my life, of my writing, challenged everything I'd learned. It challenged everything I came to see as true. It challenged beliefs, philosophies, experiences, assumptions large and small, making me re-think about everything. Not just on life; but on Healing and hope, too.

INTRODUCTION

Really, on everything *Sun* and *Wildflowers* represented to me.

I didn't want to force anything. So, like with the previous collections, I wrote as honestly as I could. Simply hoping to better understand the world around me.

Of the three, *Rain Songs* is now my favorite collection. Each one means something specific to me, as I hope they can for you too, but these words were a tether while I drifted. While we all drifted. They became a lighthouse I used to keep the land in sight; to keep the unpredictable sea from swallowing me whole. It's near impossible for me to read through them without tearing up.

2019-2021 were... well, they happened. A lot happened. Much of it was tumultuous. Political divides. Race riots. Shootings. Lockdowns. Anger. Fear. All with no end in sight. And all the while, my family and I were living abroad, far from home. A term that confused me until recently.

It was weird, living so far away; watching the world you grew up in burn.

Writing what became this collection kept me afloat. Allowing me to keep one hand on the daily pulse, with the other firmly gripped to hope. It kept me believing tomorrow was possible. That I'd get through. That we would get through, rebuild. And, eventually, the sun would rise again.

Not just because it had to. Because that's the way of things. Art followed life's current. Life has rhythms and patterns. Ups and downs. It's disruptions.

This one was just bigger than most.

Rain became the consistent metaphor naturally. Like *Sun* and *Wildflowers* before, it just fit the season. The experience.

While this may be an unpopular opinion, I've always

loved the rain. I always liked its consistency. It's rhythms. There's a dependability to it. And look at its by-products. What it produces. Lush forests. Beauty. Greenery. Flowers and blooms. Full valleys and mountainsides. Wherever rainfall is constant, life exists in abundance.

But it disrupts our preferred sunny existence. Does it not? People holiday where it's warm, often in the blistering heat, but always by water. Going somewhere tropical, but not in the rainy season.

So... *disruptive* seasons are necessary?

And we can't have those beautiful holiday seasons without some disruptive rain?

Interesting.

That challenged everything I'd come to think.

I realized the naivety of my early recovery; thinking life could be *an everlasting ray of sunshine*.

No *strife*. No *rocky seasons*.

Wouldn't that be easier? But wouldn't that lack definition? *Life*?

What need would we have for hope?

It occurred to me putting this collection together that life would always have its disruptions. They're as inevitable as the next rain, but that didn't make them bad. They simply *are*. The lens I used to see the world through, that's the imperative variable. When things happen, I can't control rain, covid, a car accident, traffic, sickness - you name it. I can lose my mind, or I can choose to use my energy more constructively.

The choice is ours, daily. There's too much at stake to waste our energy on things we can't change. It undermines our ability to change what we can.

So, though *Rain Songs* wasn't what I expected, it fit in quite well with the others. It's still about re-framing. It's

INTRODUCTION

still about choosing how one lives instead of being dragged along by crippling habits that developed. It's about choosing life and hope regardless of the situation. And it's about adaptation and change.

We hate the discomfort that comes along with life's disruptions, but most people I've talked to, looking back, cite them as the defining turning points in their lives that they'd never take back.

I hope you enjoy *Rain Songs* and that it speaks to your experiences. I hope it lifts you and encourages you, and despite the damp and somber tones of its cover, fills you with warmth as if you're sitting around a fire with friends.

Thanks for reading. Here's to normalizing conversations about mental health!

Craig Randall
March 2023

RAIN SONGS

Rain Song

continuous
stream,
endowing
life from
heaven's heights

I look up
and sing

Morning Mist

let peace fall
like morning mist,
gentle and calm

An Anchor

each drop is an
anchor, an everlasting
and forgiving spring

Tightrope

rain dances across
the tightrope of my mind,
pulling 'pon soft mem'ries

Each Drop Falls

listen as each drop
falls with gentle grace, to
lay our fears to rest

Beauty of Spring Rain

the sun, too, at times
gives way for tears to fall—the
beauty of spring rain

A Good, Heavy Rain

a good heavy rain
is somet'mes all that's needed to
clear my muddled mind

After Such Seasons: a tanka

at times, I am like
the soil after seasons
of no rain, shriveled
and parched; one pinning for thirst;
without, and in such great need

I Sing My Need For Sunlight, Warm

At times, when clouds refuse to fade,
The heart constricts at prisons made,
No hope there feels for coming storm—
My soul will sing for sunlight, warm.

When if can't feel, I, sun on skin,
Ev'n shines it does, though not within—
How to create such hopes, or form
 My soul to sing for sunlight, warm.

Even now, as dark does close
Itself upon me to impose,
Rest on hope—*this* fight's the norm:
My soul *will* sing for sunlight, warm.

Life Span

drops cascade
and flow
unseen—earthly
gravitations–until
that sudden
and final,
culminating
stop.

Lean In

I've learned not to run
from rain, to lean into the
seasons' peaceful whims

Tears Falling

the rains are but
tears falling from an
overburdened sky

Without You

without you
their hearts won't bloom,
beauty dims with lights too few;
without you
they're starved for new,
ever waiting in hopeful wombs;
without you
their hearts won't bloom.

We Mustn't Keep the Rain from Falling

We mustn't keep the rain from falling,
for risk of what we would disrupt.
Both flesh and earth would each come calling,
we mustn't keep the rain from falling.
Holding in will i'crease dissolving
and the end will quake and come, abrupt;
we mustn't keep the rain from falling,
for risk of what we would disrupt.

Rhythms of the Rain

the sun sets as I
sit ruminating on the
rhythms of the rain

Hope Drinks Deep

each drop brings
such constancy of life,
hope drinks deep

Summer Fires

summer fires burn
for days on end, no signs
of rains in sight

Speaks It's Own Truth

say what you will
about the rain, at least it
speaks its own truth

Gravity's Attempts

take offs through falling
rain, gravity's attempts won't
e'er keep me grounded

Every Footfall

I hear my heart in
every footfall of the rain,
within each and every drop

Listen Long

I listen long
while each drop carries through the sky.
I listen long
as each drop falls, and sings its song;
each drop explodes but never dies,
each one faces fate, but ne'er hides.
I listen long.

Lay Our Fears to Rest

listen as each drop
falls with gentle grace to
lay our fears to rest

Live Between

we each live somewhere
in between the starting and the
stopping of the rain

Keys

hold both sun and rain
in separate hands, and still
you hold the keys to hope

To Trust

I must learn to trust
again, step out into that
cool and calming rain

Some Days, the Rain

some days, the rains hang
heavy in the air, holding
to their hopes of flight

In Your Scars

I see your story
in your scars but feel it's truth
in every drop of rain

They Rains Will Always Fall
The skies, they brood, they break and crumble,
Without warning
The rains will fall.

Come mid-day, evening or morning,
Sound the alarm
The clouds are storming.

Whether cities, towns or farms,
Where'er you live
Protect from harm;

Be ready for what skies can bring,
But don't forget
To live, to sing.

Don't forget to breath, to leap,
Trees so pliant
So rarely weep.

Hands together, stand defiant–
The skies, they brood, they break and crumble;
Together, hope will hold, reliant–
The rains will *always* fall.

Better for the Land

let each tear drop fall;
there's nothing better for the
land than a good rain

AUTUMN AND SNOW

Glory Sets Fire

summer fades as
glory sets fire to the fall,
green erupts in gold

Love and Loss

the leaves are turning
once again, speaking, always,
of both love and loss

Magic in the Air

late autumn sunrise
scent of magic in the air
all is possible

Canvas Clean

each year, the earth will
wipe it's canvas clean; it
will begin anew

Season's Bow

early autumn rain
reveals the turning of the sun,
season takes it's bow

Gentle Turn

nature begins its
slow and gentle turn, hearts call
for rest, well-earned

Leaves Twirl

fading leaves twirl
on the path as I ride past,
dancing unaware

Not Yet Fallen

each leaf basks, no
longer ripe—not yet fallen—
resting and still

Acceptance

the trees accept that
they will lose their leaves, and fade
before their grand r'turn

Each Leaf Turns

feel the vibrant pulse
as it echoes off the wind,
each leaf turns, then falls

The Great Oak

green leaves fade to gold;
the great oak bears it's bright crown
n'gives in to the cold

No Longer Fits

like the autumn leaves,
shed what skin no longer fits;
prepare for bright'r skies

Certain Thoughts: a tanka

like the leaves, certain
thoughts must be allowed to fall,
allowed to drift
and break away,
considered then—let go

True Peace: a tanka

is true peace not found
in the knowledge that each leaf
will fall, yet still we
stand—assured of their rebirth—
acknowledging such beauty

Wilder Threads

each variant hue
calls out, tugging upon
my wilder threads

Autumn Wind Returns

at last, the autumn
wind returns to soothe, easing
all weary souls

Late Leaves

trees cling to their late
leaves, holding to the end of
season to be whole

Let Yourself Grow Bare

sometimes it's best to
let yourself grow bare, to shed
what you no longer need

Sifting

a warm autumn wind
blows through, sifting the fallen
leaves in search of warmth

Mosaic

nature's mosaic,
made as autumn's beauty bleeds,
bidding us farewell

Clinging

there I go again,
clinging to those leaves which
only wish to fall

Autumn's Light

autumn's light may lose
it's strength, but never will it
lose it's hopeful heart

Autumn's Last Leaf Lifts

autumn's last leaf lifts
even as if falls, as we
hold to promised hope

Each new Seed

all the leaves are gone,
but in their place is planted
each new seed of spring

Scarves and Tuques

wool scarves and tuques pulled
tightly over head, we make
ready for the cold

Marks a Time

it's never the end,
winter merely marks a time
of moving on

Winter's Morning Sun

winter's morning sun,
though weak, will always breach those
winding branches—for you

Winter's Weakest Sun

even the winter's
weakest sun brings warmth, and light
enough for life

Incumbent

winter is a rest
that nature needs, incumbent
for the light of life

Nature, Too

in winter, nature,
too, must seek for solitude
resting as it needs

Rehabilitation

winter is for rest,
for rehabilitation;
let the mind grow strong

NATURAL

Two Winds Converge

two winds converge at
differing pressure and speed,
conflicts then ensue

Chrysalis

a chrysalis should
be confining; it is the
pressure that refines

An Observation

a heron waits,
such mastery of stillness,
unsuspecting prey

Pure and Light

nature knows not
hatred in its soul; it's heart
is pure and light

Water Stirs

water stirs as
winds pass overhead,
revealing

Soft and Gentle

my mind at east,
giving into the the rhythm
of that soft and gentle breeze

Just Enough to Bloom

a flower takes up
no more space than it needs,
just enough to bloom

A Flower's Beauty

a flower's beauty
blooms firstly for itself;
standing tall all on its own

These Gentle, Lapping Waves Will Crash and Lull Me Off to Sleep

These gentle, lapping waves will crash and lull me off to sleep,
Carry'ng with them echoes of the sun across both day and night,
They usher in such peace—such rest—so rooted in the deep.

Some days are filled with tensions—difficulties that we reap,
Must learn let go of straining pull—need keep such hopes in sight,
These gentle, lapping waves will crash and lull me off to sleep.

When focus bends toward rhythmic breaks, the ocean's heart does keep,
For us, the peace and calm we seek, stretched over each wave's height;
They usher in such peace—such rest—so rooted in the deep.

From salty air to sun-kissed skin, the warmth of day will seep
Deep into the depth of soul, and makes perceptions right—
These gentle, lapping waves will crash and lull me off to sleep

Each worry from the day before will slip from highest steep,

Submerge themselves beneath the weight of calming shades the light;
They usher in such peace—such rest—so rooted in the deep.

Stave off whatever weary thoughts invade, infuse oneself with bright,
The sand between my toes—sea breeze—protections in the fight;
These gentle, lapping waves will crash and lull me off to sleep;
They usher in such peace—such rest—so rooted in the deep.

Wise Oaks

wise oaks grow steady,
reaching deep soil, thus will
survive the storm

Promises Fulfilled

the trees are no
longer bare, fulfilling their
promise once again

An Unexpected Spring Snow

an unexpected
spring snow—to some, a gift of
imagination

Hibiscus

sweet scents of summer
hang upon the welcome breeze,
hibiscus in bloom

Daffodils

daffodils won't sprout
before their time is due; they wait
knowing birth is *true*

Upstream

paths become unclear,
healing isn't linear,
some steps lead upstream

STORMS AND SKYLINES

Thunder Claps

thunder claps,
severing mass from mass,
mind from body

Insecurities

insecurities
resurface, undermining
contented natures

Exhaustion Lumbers

exhaustion lumbers,
like the soft coming of clouds,
sneakily setting in

Heavy is the Heart

heavy is the heart of
those who bare the weight of mind,
who hope for clearer skies

Born to Weather

we were born to
weather storms and endure
'til clear skies come

Chance the Skies

we are limited
only by our fear to fall;
we must chance the skies

Choose to Believe

lift your eyes to see,
choose to believe; clouds break as
light begins to stream

More

what if the sky
maintained it was nothing more
than it's last storm

The Mind pt 3 -- Inevitable Evacuations

dams burst,
filling the
flood plains
below

populated
areas need
be ready for
evacuation

Unexpected Storms

insecurities
flare when infiltrated by
unexpected storms

In Wrath

what crippling weight
is there in wrath, an all
consuming fire

My hopes I hold abreast, as treasures in my heart

My hopes I hold abreast, as treasures in my heart,
Tighter grasp, I cling and clutch, while dusk assumes its rite,
I will endure these shadows, 'til all my ghosts depart.

As spectres hold and haunt me still, I steady to my part,
As anchors hold, I won't be moved, nor ever forced to flight
My hopes I hold abreast, as treasures in my heart.

Such fears will shape themselves as will to prey upon such art,
Such schemes designed, defences strong, to weary any might
I will endure these shadows, 'til all my ghosts depart.

Their hopes they fling to overwhelm, beg my despair to start,
Direct my thoughts to victories, past memories ignite,
My hopes I hold abreast, as treasures in my heart.

To isolate is fear's first goal, while maps of hope un-chart,
Hold fast, I must, to Love's sure hold, in getting through the night
I will endure these shadows, 'til all my ghosts depart.

E'en at its darkest stretch, when dawn is yet revealed in sight,
When ghostly shadows all consume, converge on me with fight,
My hopes I hold abreast, as treasures in my heart,
I will endure these shadows, 'til all my ghosts depart.

Wind is Plenty Wise

wind is plenty wise,
passing over and around
needless obstacles

The Way is Forward

the way is forward
through each storm, through wind and rain;
these will always pass

Hear Such Secrets Spilled

be still and hear such
secrets spilled, peaceful whispers
of the gentle wind

Invade

insecurities
invade with sudden shifts—the
changing of the guard

Still Can't See

still can't see ahead,
but I will face what fears I
find and overcome

Confining Ceiling

those skies were not but
a confining ceiling, built
to comfort others

Baptized

be baptized by the
storm; let it strike you and rile—
guide you on your way

Edge of the World

edge of the world,
where sky sinks into sea, I
find myself in b'tween

Their Own Voice

storms speak not for the
sun, for both hold true to the
strength of their own voice

Other Winds

inconsequential
are the whims of other winds,
when one's choice is clear

Greet Yourself with Grace

when tomorrow feels
lost in fog, remember to
greet yourself with grace

Some Say

some say we were born
to bend and fold and break—I
know this t'be untrue

Clear

head full of clear sky,
winds sail smoothly once again,
my course corrected

AT FIRST LIGHT

Bold Horizon's Fire

can you see it,
the coming of the dawn,
bold horizon's fire

Light Breaks Through

light breaks through the trees,
gentle morning reminders
of hope, what each new day brings

Expectant

let the early morning
sculpt for you new reasons to
believe—*expectant*

No Longer Cast

at last, I heed that
hope has healed, for day's no
longer cast in night

Lest We Miss the Coming Dawn

be careful not to let
the night stir fear, lest we
miss the coming dawn

Lift Our Gaze and See

even as the sun
does rise, 'tis up to us to
lift our gaze and see

Bursting

see the morning once
again, bursting at the seams
with its bright beauty

New Light Dawns

new light dawns, yet
still I find it hard in heart
to trust it now

Tomorrow's Canvas

tomorrow's canvas
is still clean, ready and ripe
for you to dream

Threads of Hope

I see them in the
setting and the rising of
the sun, threads of hope

Beauty Echoes

such beauty echoes
'cross the sky; calling forth my
soul from its deep sleep

Morning's Fire

don't you think the night
grows weary, too, and yearns to
burn with morning's fire

Far From Mind

sunup sometimes feels
so much further from the mind
than the time it takes to rise

A Simple Sunrise

a simple sunrise
often will remind—hearts can
be made whole again

THE LAST LIGHT OF DAY

Evening Light

her light is softer,
setting gentle fire to
the waters as we pass

Day Comes to a Close

light touches down
upon the horizon line,
day comes to a close

A Cup of Tea

cup of tea at dusk,
as the sky's full color fades,
settling the mind

Waiting for the Night

the moon, too, has need
to rise, yet rests by day's light,
waiting for the night

Unobstructed

unobstructed,
the crisp and cool night air
brings clarity

Countless

countless are they in
number, flick'ring and brilliant
little lights—our thoughts

Still and Quiet Calm

the night sky stirs in
me a still and quiet calm,
bringing needed rest

Beneath the Silence

can you feel it,
solace beneath the
silence of the moon

Pyres

pyres steeped in past,
strike the match and watch the flames
climb high'r and high'r

Restless Nights

my spirit is
stronger—I *know*—and will 'ndure
these restless nights

Rising of the Sun

no amount of
shadow will ever halt the
rising of the sun

Moon or Mars

to the moon or mars,
keep your imagination
rooted in the stars

Hope is a Friend

hope is a friend who
holds you close and bares with you
through ev'ry lonely night

Light Fades Early

the light fades early
this time of year, but day gives
way for stars to shine

New Constellations

tear down the stars if
you need, rebuild; make room for
new constellations

Til Dawn

the night sky sheds its
own light, enough for us to
see our steps til dawn

Two Souls Collide

two souls collide
in this lonely world, setting
fire to the dark

Magic Hangs Upon the Night

magic hangs upon
the night sky; when I look up
I am revived

HAIKU FOR HUMAN RIGHTS

Roofs Will Only Keep

roofs will only keep
us from the rain if equal
is their reach for all

Until Every Heart is Free

until every heart
is free, we are trapped living
in a crippled past

Inequality

inequality
runs rampant when eyes are blind,
wake up to the noise

Every Single Person

no soul is free
until *every single person*
can reach the same stars

Youth Rising

voices of the youth
rising like the ocean waves
readying themselves to break

One More Soul Falls

as one more soul falls,
defense for culprits deafens;
what's it going to take

Ethics

these savage means
used to hold so many down;
ethics *lost at sea*?

Breathe and Bleed

all breathe and bleed
the same'n share such wondrous hopes,
f'r'now undone by hate

In the Margins

love lingers longer
in the margins, for those whose
heads hang low

Or Can Be

I feel the subtle changes
in the wind, progress' true drive;
futures—still—are bright

Fear Clouds All Reason

fear clouds all reason
angry mobs assume control;
are we all the same

The Way Back

the way back will not
be clear and will require much
patient understanding

A People Rising

feel the
fierceness
of those
who will not
be held
down

burning
eruptions
rise

Bullets Fly as Bodies Fall

at a loss once more
bullets fly as bodies fall
still no end in sight

Children's Children

and where will we tell
our children's children that we
stood when justice failed

BEACONS

No Flame in Hand

hope is a fire
kindled with no flame in hand,
empty, sparked by need

Unwavering

unwavering is
the strength of hope—its shine and
its audacity

The Mind pt 4

shadows
cling like
soggy rags
on stone,
suffocating—

prayers
sift up'wards,
emergent
light

Let Hope Be What Lifts

let hope be what lifts
us high and rights the course of
wayward steps gone wrong

Yet To Feel

step into your strength,
you have yet to feel or find
the pow'r which waits with'n

Light the Beacons

light the beacons;
send those signal flares to sky
so help will come

Watchfires

don't you worry, friend,
we'll keep the watchfires lit and
wait with you til dawn

Indestructible

once again, it has
tested true—the *hope* I hold,
indestructible

Let Love Lift

let love lift you when
your strength has failed and carry
you to calmer shores

Sure to Come

shake off those shadows
that are sure to come; let the
light within you burn

In the Way It Binds

forgiveness, mortar
in the way it binds, unites
what can will strong 'gain

Still Its Shine

the sun can still its
shine as it chooses; burning
for its own beauty

Love's Labors

true love's labors will
lift and make work light, filling
all the world with worth

Authenticity

the world's in desp'rate
need of authenticity,
our*selves* shining through

Sun Upon My Skin

once more, I feel the
need for sun upon my skin,
all its hopeful warmth

Hope Is

hope is what burns so
deep within, setting fire to
spirit, mind and soul

Of Good Courage

be of good courage
let not the light of each new
day be wasted

INTENTIONS

A Harvest

not every day can
hold a harvest, sometimes we
need to till the land

Pump the Breaks

pump the breaks,
this world ain't slowing down
on its own account

Synapses

sever those synapses
that add weight to mind; only
feed what thoughts will lift

Make Yourself Light

nothing lifts like a
thankful heart; so make yourself
light and lend a hand

Hold Your Head Up High

hold your head up high;
your countenance will follow;
hope will always rise

Just Let Go

why carry around
what we no longer need when
we can just let go

To Discredit

heaviness pulls at
my posture; moving itself
to discredit progress

Familiar Slide

I've been here before,
in this same familiar slide;
creeping doubts I *won't* abide

Cataclysmic

cataclysmic can
be the depth of loss if love's
left unresolved

Weapon of the Weak

shame is a weapon
of the weak, of those who fail
to grasp how hearts are won

Labels Breed Reality

be careful what you
let sink deep, for labels
breed reality

Currents Strengthen Speed

hold fast when currents
strengthen speed, they need not
alter our direction

I Must Break Free

These bars are strong
I must break free
This cage, unlawful, wrong.
These bars are strong
This sentence long
My mind has been deceived–
These bars are strong
I must break free

Before We Break

like the ocean waves,
we can only hold so long
before we break

Reconcile

reconcile the past'n
r'move what anchors hold you back;
ready yourself to fly

Strength of Hope

steadfast is the strength
of hope, and sturdy when we
find ourselves in need

Shoulder of a Friend

there is no strength like
the shoulder of a friend, that
holds up heavy hearts

Mark

a conversation
with a friend is sometimes all
a heart needs to heal

Shoulder to Shoulder

shoulder to shoulder,
that's how we're going to make it through,
together, always

Reminded Once More

reminded once more
of much needed time away,
regroup, refresh—*breathe*

Power In You

there is power in
you yet, much more than you've been
led to understand

Forecast

despite the forecast
tomorrow is a blank page
to be written as one wills

Through Soil

we must learn to see
b'yond *the impossible*,
like seeds through soil

The Mind pt. 5

it is
we who
till the
soil rich

who
choose which
plants to
thrive

Kindness

be patient
with yourself, acting—*always*—
in kindness

Life's Rhythm Returns

life's rhythm returns,
as—once more, the horizon
feels within my reach

A Soul Awake

to see a flower
in full bloom is to see a
soul alive, awake

Innocence Regained

making snow angels
in the cool, crisp morning air,
innocence regained

The Course a River Flows

we can change the course
a river goes but never
halt its rushing flow

Quiet Intention

rest upon what
cultivated peace you've won,
quiet intention

Stillness is an Art

stillness is an
art I know I have further
need to grow

Room to Breathe

remove the clutter
from 'midst confining walls,
set *this* room to breathe

Foliage

the roads are littered
with foliage from the storm,
still, we'll have them cleared

Unfinished Book

cup of tea resting
on my nightstand, next to my
unfinished book

BOUNDARY LINES

True North

if true north leads me
east, I will brave those paths
with utmost trust and truth

Evident Boundaries

nature has no true
bridal, but there exists—with'n—
evident boundaries

The Mind pt. 6 — Thinking Clear

the earth quakes
beneath, shaking,
splintering cracks
undermine sure
footing

clear
thoughts emerge
in-force

Wreckage

survey the wreckage
find what parts can be salvaged
carry on with repairs

What Space You Need

take what space you need,
healing comes as hope can breathe,
healthy boundaries

Cooler Climates

summer's sweat builds on
my brow as I go in search
of cooler climates

Lost and Found

I am somewhere
'twixt the beauty of being
both lost and found

Inch By Inch

make your bound'ries clear,
or they will take, inch by inch,
til all the space is...

Circling

circling, I've been
searching wide and far for such
a place to land

Overgrown

the path lies ahead,
half-covered and overgrown
but ready for you

Far From Done

look back and see and
remember how far you've come;
you are far from done

Time to Rebuild

time to rebuild,
reforge our paths to peace,
and hopes distilled

Reset the Foundations

it's time to rebuild,
to reset the foundations
and cast my hopes fulfilled

Into Your Strength

step into your strength;
you have yet to feel or find
the pow'r that waits with'n

TRANSFORMATIONS

A Myth

there's a myth
that what is broken cannot
be remade

Torn In Two

to be at odds with
self is the epitome of
living torn in two

Truth that Severs

unsettling is
the truth that severs belief,
sewing uncertainty

Pay No Mind

pay no mind to
doubts, for never have they
been a friend of yours

Dreams of Change

the cage became too
comfortable as dream of change
felt far too far away

Agent of Change

I am my own
agent of change, harnessed
by no other

If Needs Arise

rip those roots
right from the soil, harsh
if needs arise

Seeking Habitation

without form,
spirits seek for h'bitation,
lingering alone

Wrong Question

what if 'who am I?'
is the wrong question; rather
'who will I become?'

Bravery

bravery is
learning to let go, baring
one's self to *be*

In Transit

upon the
threshold, in transit
from one
moment to
the next

I reach out

Hopes are Sewn

speak, then let it grow;
what we choose to think will root,
roads to hope are sewn

Feel Life's Pulse

I want to go
someplace that I've never been
and feel life's pulse

Know That We Can Fly

if we never leap
we'll never get the chance to
know that we can fly

Dare to Dream

dare to dream,
be audacious and
expectant

This Heart Ain't Broken

this heart ain't broken,
maybe worn and bruised but
strong enough to fly

Many Forms of Medicine

there are many forms
of medicine, laught'r and love,
and that which lifts above

Fortress

my heart is a
fortress, built not of stone but
of belief, and strong

Stories Old

recite for me those
stories old, those tales when told
will lift my spirit

Keeps Your Feet Aground

let hope be stronger
than what ails your heart, than what
keeps your feet aground

Gratitude's Great Gift

in these troubled times
giving thanks can lift our grief,
gratitude's great gift

The Verge

on the verge
the edge
of
what will
be

potential
pure
exacting
once
unleashed

for now it
sits at
rest
waiting
-
waiting
to
soar

to *be.*

Rest the Oars

rest the oars,
let the current run while we
lay back and drift

Memorial Stones

hold on to cherished
tokens collected o'er time,
memorial stones

YOU WITH ME

Wonders

let's go wandering,
let's get lost and see what
wonders we can find

Sweeter Than

waking up with you,
sweeter than a sunrise
lighting up the dawn

Heartbeats of My Life

slow Sunday mornings
sipping my coffee with you,
heartbeats of my life

Gravity's Sure Grip

comfort comes as your
eyes stare through mine—reminders of
gravity's sure grip

Masks

it was for you I
first removed the mask, hoping
to be understood

You Took My Hand

thankful for those times
you took my hand—those times I
lost the strength needed to stand

Together

together, we will
make it through, and endure the
season's subtle change

Beneath the Sun

I want to sit with
you beneath the sun and feel
it's warm embrace

Never Wavering

your strength I see,
it streams through every day,
never wavering

Long Walks With You

long walks with you,
with no set destination,
lift my spirit high

By Water's Edge

tranquil scenes approach,
you and I by water's edge,
sun sinks in the sky

A Walk With You

a walk with you
among the sunlit fields,
my heart is full

Leaving the Light On

thank you my love, my
hope and my heart, for leaving
the light on for me

All Night With You

I'll stay up all night
with you to see those very
first few streaks of dawn

Some Days are Marked by Sun and Some by Rain

Some days are marked by sun and some by rain;
Both, *still*, can strain as much as they can lift.
But any day I spend with you remains
A day that I will always count: *a gift.*

Sometimes the skies will threaten us with tears,
And over years the rivers choose to rise,
But in the end, it's love that o'vercomes'r fears;
It's love amidst the madness that defies.

Even when the fields are dried 'n'turn to dust,
Or when the Trust of Old's in short supply,
Faith in the love we've built—*before*—we must
Hold to, for its foundations we rely.

Always, I'll take your hand in sun or rain
And fuel a love no sky could e'er hope contain.

AFTERWORD

First off, thank you for reading. These words were lifelines for me during a tumultuous time. I hope they encouraged and lifted you. I wanted to leave you with a list of reminders, things this strange season reminded me:

- Life goes up and down; but always forward. We should too.
- Healing isn't Linear.
- Healing doesn't happen in isolation. Find your people and love fiercely.
- Hope is strong.
- You/I/We are strong.
- It's okay not to be okay.
- Life is supposed to ebb and flow.
- Follow your own convictions.
- Relax, lean in, and enjoy each moment; what we take as *bad* is fodder for growth
- And life is about growth. (That's always a beautiful thing).

AFTERWORD

Thank you for reading. Thank you for hoping. Thank you for your part in the conversation about mental health, healing, and making space for people to grapple with our ever-changing world. Remember: you're powerful and strong and already have everything you need within you to confront whatever haunts your mind. Breath and smile. Find people who let you be authentic. And live!

Also, Covid decimated the roots my family laid down abroad, resulting in us moving back home to be near family. This did something interesting. It forced me to reconcile why I moved away in the first place. In doing so, gave me an opportunity to confront my original scars, leading to some of the deepest and most imperative healing of my life. All of which is chronicled in a follow up collection, *Coming Home*. Due out in 2024.

Printed in the USA
CPSIA information can be obtained
at www.ICGtesting.com
LVHW042010270923
759498LV00014B/35/J

JOIN THE NEWSLETTER